Seeing Stars

Written by
Jill Atkins

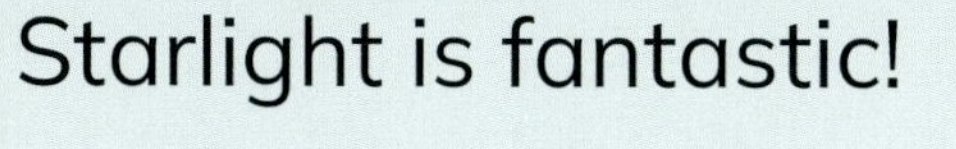

Starlight is fantastic!

To see the stars, you need a clear, dark night with no moon.

You must stand as far from lights as you can.

Look up!

Can you see hundreds
and hundreds of stars?

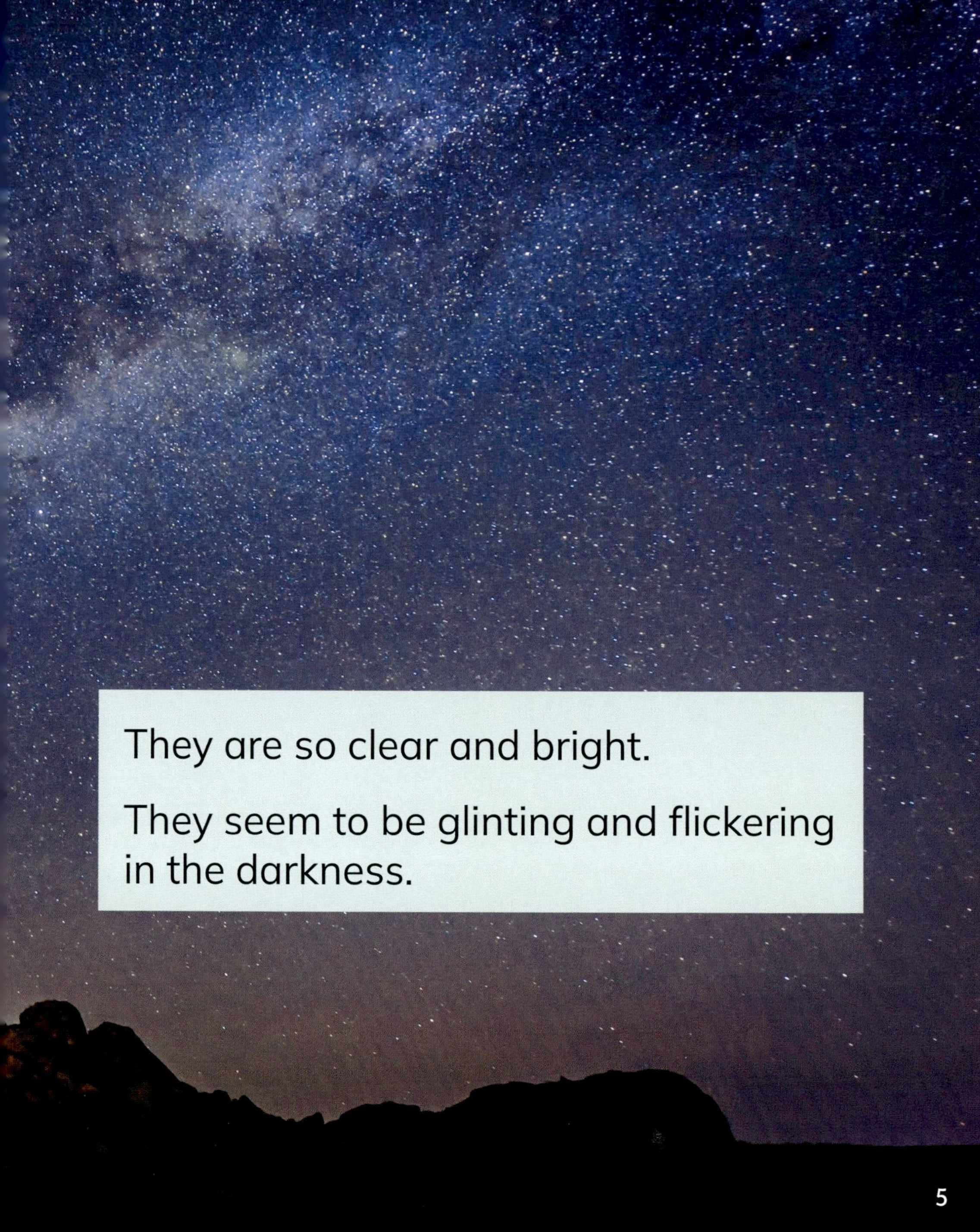

They are so clear and bright.

They seem to be glinting and flickering in the darkness.

With luck, you might see some shooting stars too.

Look! There is one. Do not blink or you will miss it.

Some stars you can see are in fact not stars at all. They are **planets**!

Stars are distant from us, but planets are near.

This is **Mars**, the red planet.

Some stars seem to form patterns.

This cluster of stars looks like
a hunter.

This one looks like twins. Or do you see a dog? Or a pair of goats?

You must join the dots to see a pattern.

Do you think this looks like a cooking pan?

It is the **Big Dipper**.

Some stars are brighter than the rest.

If you sail on a ship, the bright stars can help you get back to land.

See if you can spot some of the patterns on a clear, dark night.

This might help you see them better!